Original title:
Lavender Legends

Copyright © 2025 Creative Arts Management OÜ
All rights reserved.

Author: Jameson Hartfield
ISBN HARDBACK: 978-1-80566-769-8
ISBN PAPERBACK: 978-1-80566-839-8

Whispers of the Scented Wind

In the garden, a bee made a dance,
Twirling around, with a joyful prance.
Whispers of flowers, secrets they share,
Buzzing along, without a care.

The breezes giggle, they tickle our noses,
As petals keep trading their silly poses.
In this funny realm, birds chirp in glee,
Where even the toads sing harmoniously.

A cat thinks it's all just a game,
Chasing its tail as if it were fame.
Scented stories float through the air,
While frogs in tuxedos dance without care.

So come, take a whiff, have a laugh or two,
In this marigold maze where nothing is true.
Life's a bouquet, bursting with cheer,
Join the hilarity, there's nothing to fear!

Secrets in the Blooming Silence

Amidst the petals, a gnome takes a nap,
Dreaming of gardens and a flowing tap.
The daisies giggle, they add their spin,
They'd tell us all, if only they'd grin.

A snail with a top hat, oh what a sight,
Says it prefers stargazing at night.
While butterflies whisper their craziest lore,
They claim every thought opens a door!

In corners where daisies decide to bicker,
The sunflowers argue who's the best flicker.
A reason to chuckle, a reason to smile,
All while counting the bees in a pile.

Beneath the silence, the laughter runs deep,
In secretive gardens where critters don't sleep.
So tiptoe on petals, partake in the fun,
For nature's a jester when day's nearly done!

The Violet Tides

Waves of violets crash with a cheer,
Sending sweet scents, oh so near.
As colors collide in a playful race,
Each bloom wears a grin, a comical face.

The tides of laughter blend with the sea,
Where jellyfish jive in a wobbly spree.
Each splash and giggle makes flowers sway,
As crabs tap dance, in a sea cabaret.

Seashells tell tales of shimmering bright,
Of fish in tuxedos, what a delight!
So grab your straw hat and join in the fun,
In this violet tide under the sun.

With giggling waves and mischievous airs,
Nature's a jester, do you dare?
To dance with the petals and work up a rhyme,
In the realm of the violet, it's always prime!

Tales of Aromatic Rebirth

Once a plain seed, it longed for a twist,
Planted in soil with not much to assist.
Then came the sunshine, a sprinkle of rain,
And out popped a bloom, oh what a gain!

The flowers conspire, the roots start to laugh,
Declaring the sprout a new photograph.
With petals so bright, it struts down the lane,
In a comedy show of humorous reign.

Bees come for selfies, what a silly crowd,
Beaming with joy, they buzz oh so loud.
With every petal's twist and each little twirl,
The garden's a stage for the sprouting whirl.

So here's to rebirth, in colors so bold,
Where every flower has tales to be told.
Join the parade, let laughter expand,
In this fragrant fiesta, take a stand!

Whispers Among the Petals

In fields where purple dreams reside,
The bees all gather, filled with pride.
They dance and buzz in silly glee,
While flowers giggle, "Look at me!"

The rabbits hop, with grace and flair,
Sporting tiny hats and quite a dare.
They tell their jokes in hushed delight,
While stars above twinkle goodnight.

Legends Woven in Scent

A squirrel once claimed he could out-snooze,
In a lavender blanket, he'd never lose!
His friends just laughed, a playful tease,
"Wake up, you fluffy, it's time for cheese!"

With each new story, the petals sway,
As critters argue, "It's my turn today!"
They weave their tales through the fragrant air,
And roll in the bed of the flowers fair.

The Veil of the Violet Night

When nighttime falls with a purple glow,
The fireflies gather, putting on a show.
They flicker and flash like disco lights,
While owls clap wings, adding to the sights.

In a quiet whisper, the moon does tease,
As raccoons dance beneath the trees.
"Who will take the prize for best moonwalk?"
The crickets chirp, the stars just gawk.

Harmony in Floral Melodies

The frogs once formed a singing band,
With frogs on drums and a flower stand.
They croaked their tunes with grand aplomb,
And bugs flew free in a sweetly calm.

With petals swaying, the frogs felt bold,
Each note they sang was worth its weight in gold.
A joyous party in scented air,
Where all are welcome, laughter to share.

The Guardians of the Aromatic World

In fields of purple, they stand so tall,
Their scent spread laughter, enchanting all.
With capes made of petals, they take their flight,
Guarding quirky dreams from morning till night.

They tickle the noses of sleepy goats,
While squirrels debate, wearing tiny coats.
The guardians giggle, twirling around,
In their fragrant realm where joy can be found.

The Enchanter's Purple Palette

An enchanter with colors, a mischievous art,
Danced with a brush and stole every heart.
He painted the skies in shades of delight,
Then slipped on a banana peel, oh what a sight!

His palette of purple spilled giggles and cheer,
Bubbling over with joy, it was clear.
He laughed as the flowers began to sway,
Creating wild jokes throughout the whole day.

Tales of the Enchanted Herb

Once there was a herb, quite funky and green,
Who played silly pranks, always a scene.
It whispers to daisies and sprinkles its charm,
With every soft giggle, it means no alarm.

Its tales get shared at the moonlit night,
Where bunnies abound, with laughter in flight.
They twirl in the breeze, both silly and spry,
As the enchanted herb gives a wink to the sky.

Revelations in the Purple Whisper

A purple whisper floated past the old fence,
Making even the grumpy start feeling intense.
It giggled through breezes, bringing a cheer,
Turning heads of even the crankiest deer.

The flowers conspired, with gossip to spread,
As bees buzzed around, their tiny frames fed.
In the heart of the dusk, with laughter so wild,
The purple whisper played, like a mischievous child.

Dusk and Dew

In fields of purple, the bees do dance,
A clumsy fly joins, but lacks some grace.
It tumbles and rolls, as if in a trance,
And bumps the bee's head, oh what a face!

The sun dips low, the moon takes its place,
A rabbit hops in, with quite a show.
He slips, he flips, in a comical race,
With a wiggly tail and a wink of 'hello!'

The night air giggles, the stars now jest,
As crickets chirp tunes that make us grin.
The moonlight's laughter, it feels like a fest,
In the land of blooms, let the fun begin.

So join the circus of dusk's sweet whim,
Where every petal has stories to tell.
In twilight's glow, and shadows that brim,
Adventure awaits, who knew this so well?

Lavender Shadows

Amidst the flowers, shadows prance,
A frog tries ballet, oh what a sight!
He leaps and he flops, with little chance,
Yet thinks he's the star of this lavender night.

A wise old owl hoots, with a smirk,
As the frog takes a bow, and slips in the dew.
But nature just chuckles, it's all just a perk,
In the grand theater where oddities grew.

With giggles from petals and whispers of breeze,
The grass joins in, tickling toes of the bees.
And when the moon chuckles, it's hard not to freeze,
In the comedic night of bizarre mysteries.

So if you wander where shadows play,
Bring your sense of humor, and join the fun.
For every bloom hides a tale, night or day,
In this wacky wonder, there's laughter for everyone!

The Aromatic Journeys

Through fields of whimsy, aromas swirl,
A skunk holds a sign that says 'potpourri'.
With a sniff and a giggle, he joins the whirl,
In the chaotic dance of this fragrant spree.

The bees wear tiny hats, quite a sight,
Buzzing in harmony, what a fun crew!
While fireflies twinkle, adding delight,
They flash like disco balls, as night bids adieu.

A squirrel in shades thinks he's a star,
He struts through the plants, with daring flair.
But stumbles and tumbles, not going far,
And lands on a patch that's beyond compare.

With laughter erupting from petals so bold,
And scents that tickle, oh what a thrill!
In this aromatic realm, let joy unfold,
Join the expedition, and catch the festive chill!

Violet Hues of Myth

Legends they weave, where purple reigns,
A warrior cat prances, sword held high.
But trips on a root, oh what strange pains,
As he scales the kingdom, with a lowly sigh.

A wizard in robes made of flowers bright,
Tries casting spells with a lavender wand.
But every great spell goes a bit awry,
And turns all his potions to candy beyond!

With fireflies buzzing, they laugh in the night,
As frogs don hats and the hedgehogs parade.
This world of oddities, oh what a sight,
Where every bloom's story leads to charades.

So if you believe in tales quite absurd,
Join in the fun, embrace every whim.
For amidst all the purple, you'll find the word,
That legends are laughter — let's sing and swim!

The Essence of a Flowered Secret

In gardens where the flowers play,
A buzzing bee just lost his way.
He danced around a purple hue,
And whispered tales we never knew.

The petals giggled in the breeze,
Sharing secrets with great ease.
They plotted pranks and tricks galore,
Like hiding socks behind the door.

A ladybug wore shades so bright,
Claiming she was quite the sight.
But in the sun she turned too red,
And had to bury her sweet head.

With every breeze, a ticklish laugh,
As flowers penned their secret craft.
In every sprout and sprig so small,
Their funny stories charm us all.

Melodies of the Fragrant Night

At dusk the blooms began to sing,
With crickets chirping as they swing.
The moonlight cast a purple glow,
As frogs joined in the garden show.

A hedgehog tapped a tiny beat,
While flowers danced upon their feet.
They threw a party, oh so bright,
With nectar punch and snacks just right.

A butterfly forgot his line,
And tumbled down, but looked just fine.
He shouted, 'I'm the star tonight!'
In laughter, flowers took to flight.

So if you hear a rustling sound,
In twilight where the blossoms abound,
Join in their song, don't be shy,
For little laughs will never die.

Lingering in Purple Dreams

In dreams of purple, sweet and bold,
The flowers tell their tales of old.
A squirrel with a tiny hat,
Thought he was grand, but oh, the chat!

The daisies rolled their petals tight,
And giggled at his silly plight.
'That hat is way too big,' they teased,
While he just grinned and felt quite pleased.

A snail with shades crawled past so slow,
Said, 'Watch me! I'm the star of this show!'
But fell asleep, curled up in glee,
Dreaming of a racing spree.

So linger long in dreams so bright,
Where flowers join in playful light.
Embrace the joy, the fun, the schemes,
For laughter blooms in purple dreams.

The Lure of Lilac Legends

In fields where lilacs whisper tales,
A gopher's dance left curious trails.
He juggled seeds, oh what a sight,
With twirls and swirls in the moonlight.

The lilacs laughed until they cried,
As gopher tripped and flourished wide.
He spun around, then did a flip,
Landed near a ladybug ship.

They hosted games of hop and skip,
With flowers joining in the quip.
A bumblebee played the tambourine,
While daisies cheered, so bright and green.

The night was filled with joy and cheer,
With lilacs merry, not a fear.
For every dance and playful jest,
In floral realms, they are the best.

The Magic of the Scented Moon

Under the moon, scents begin to play,
A giggling breeze joins in the fray.
Flowers wear crowns, don't they look grand?
Even the crickets form a band!

A squirrel doing dance in the light,
Twisting and turning, oh what a sight!
The owls are laughing, no need to swoon,
Just don't let the skunks join the tune!

Fireflies wink, they got jokes to spill,
As they glow while munching on dill.
The night is silly, filled with glee,
Where magic blends with harmony!

In this scented land, fun's the decree,
Where laughter and flowers run wild and free.
With every whiff, a chuckle we fetch,
Under the moon, we twirl, and we sketch!

Songs of the Purple Horizon

Over hills where the purple blooms sing,
Bees start buzzing like they're the king.
Each petal dances, a jig or two,
Twirling 'round, sporting their purple hue!

A rabbit hops, with rhythm divine,
Telling his tales, sipping on thyme.
A frog croaks loudly, adds to the mix,
While flowers take selfies – what a fix!

The sun sets slowly, casting a glow,
While clouds in the distance begin to flow.
A turtle joins in, slow as can be,
Singing a ballad, oh what a spree!

From the horizon, laughter erupts anew,
As petals and critters share what they do.
In purple delight, a joyful parade,
Where songs of the blooms never do fade!

Whispers of the Purple Field

In a field of whispers, secrets are told,
With each petal bright, like stories of old.
A dandelion dreams, with hopes held high,
While bees in the corner practice to fly!

The wind giggles soft, with nibbles of fun,
As butterflies flutter, they are never done.
The grass gets jealous, it starts to sway,
Wishing it too could dance and play!

A snail takes a look, then decides to race,
But who'd ever thought a snail could keep pace?
His shell is a carriage, round and quite sleek,
As the daisies cheer—oh, what a peak!

The sun winks brightly, the laughter resounds,
With whimsical whispers, joy knows no bounds.
In the purple field, we frolic and cheer,
With whispers and giggles, let's bring the year!

Enchanted Aroma

In a garden where aromas collide,
The air is thick with laughter and pride.
Mint jokes with basil, a spicy ballet,
While cumin cracks jokes that brighten the day!

A rose whispers sweetly, 'What's in a name?',
While thyme adds sass, igniting the flame.
With sprigs all around, there's humor so rich,
Even the carrots are starting to twitch!

A gnome tips his hat, with a twinkle in eye,
Spinning tall tales under the sky.
His friends, the weeds, poke fun and they snicker,
Says he's a gardener, but grows a sticker!

In this enchanting herb-filled spree,
Every breath reveals a giggle for free.
As aromas combine in joyous delight,
Let's dance through the garden, from morning to night!

Echoes of Floral Harmony

In a garden so bright, blooms a curious sight,
Bees gather round, buzzing with delight.
Flora in giggles, dancing with glee,
Even the breeze joins, singing wild and free.

A snail in a race, thought he could win,
But a wise old turtle said, "Just take it on the chin!"
With petals around, they both find their way,
Laughing at time as they frolic and play.

The sun wears a hat, with a wink and a grin,
While daisies shout jokes, neat and thin.
Every flower chuckles, roots full of cheer,
In this floral world, happiness is near.

So when you feel blue, and need a good laugh,
Just stroll through the blooms, take a moment to gaff.
For in every petal, there's a story to share,
Of purple giggles and scandalous air.

The Violet Pathway

A walk on the path where the violets bloom,
Children in giggles, creating a zoom.
Rabbits in bowties, throwing a ball,
While squirrels in shades, are having a ball.

Toadstools are seats for the insects' big show,
With ants clapping hands, rooting for the glow.
A frog makes a joke, ribbiting loud,
And butterflies join, swirling in a crowd.

The sun is a joker, playing hide and seek,
Tickling petals and making them squeak.
In a whirl of giggles, time floats away,
As flowers tell tales of a whimsical day.

So if you feel gray, or lost in the fray,
Just find this pathway, let laughter hold sway.
For in every moment, a chuckle can grow,
Among violets dancing, with giggles to flow.

Poets of the Purple Field

In a field of purple, poets convene,
With quills and with ink, composing a scene.
But bees play pranks, stealing the pens,
While flowers erupt in giggles and trends.

One poet, quite bold, wrote a verse so long,
The breeze whispered back, "You're doing it wrong!"
With petals in laughter, they dance and they spin,
Finding inspiration in chuckles to win.

The daisies compete for the best joke around,
While clovers in crowns prance on soft ground.
Each line that they share lifts the spirits up high,
As giggles and rhymes make the flowers all sigh.

So join in this field where the poets set free,
A bouquet of fun, wild as can be.
For in every verse, there's a lesson to glean,
That laughter is golden, and joy is the queen.

Moonlit Whispers

Underneath the moon, where the shadows play,
Flowers whisper secrets, in a cheeky way.
With giggles in petals, they share tales anew,
Of starry romances and the dew that they drew.

The nightingale croons, a comical tune,
While fireflies flicker, igniting the balloon.
Flora twirls gently, under silvery beams,
Crafting a dance made of whimsical dreams.

In this midnight garden, where mischief is sown,
The poppies tell stories that are totally blown.
With laughter as sweet as the fragrance so bold,
They weave through the night, breaking the mold.

So if ever you wander when the moon's shining bright,
Listen for whispers, in the cool of the night.
For under the stars, where the flowers convene,
Lies a world of joy that's lively and serene.

The Celestial Bloom

A flower fell from up above,
It landed where the bees all shove.
It tickled noses, made folks sneeze,
And caused a fight for buzzing bees.

In purple hues, it danced with breeze,
With colors bright, it aimed to tease.
The carrots claimed it smelled like funk,
While cows just laughed and called it junk.

But in the night, the stars would twirl,
Around the bloom, they'd spin and swirl.
They'd giggle bright, their tails aglow,
While moos and buzzes put on a show.

So if you find that flower bold,
Join in the antics, be very bold.
For laughter thrives where petals lay,
And silliness is here to stay.

Legends Written in Purple

In a land where jokes grow tall,
There lived a flower known to all.
Its petals wore a comical guise,
With laughter echoing 'neath sunny skies.

The squirrels would race, plotting their schemes,
To steal its seeds for nutty dreams.
But when they grabbed those treasures bright,
They'd trip on vines, oh what a sight!

A tale unfolds where bees aspire,
To buzz around and never tire.
With each sweet sip of nectar's kiss,
They'd join the dance in pure bliss.

So here's a yarn of purple cheer,
Where laughter blooms throughout the year.
In every petal, joy is penned,
A silly secret that won't end.

Gardens of Dreams

In gardens wild where giggles sprout,
Each flower has a funny clout.
With petals soft and dreams set free,
They plot a world of silly glee.

The rabbits wear their hats askew,
As daisies dance in shades of blue.
While butterflies bring tea for fun,
And toast the sun 'til day is done.

With plump tomatoes and giggles round,
They host a feast, the best in town.
The joke's on weeds—too shy to bloom,
While veggies waltz and flowers zoom!

So come and play, don't hesitate,
In this oddball world, it's never late.
Join in the fun, let laughter stream,
In these bright gardens of our dreams.

Carriers of Scented Shadows

This flower tells a tale each night,
Of shadowy fun and sheer delight.
It whispers secrets to the moon,
And dances lightly to a tune.

The crickets chirp, the fireflies gleam,
Around the scent, they form a team.
With every waft, the stories spread,
Of purple dreams that must be fed.

The owls are wise, they tip their hats,
As naughty foxes chase their chats.
While raccoons laugh and hope to pry,
The essence hidden in the sky.

So if you chance upon this flower,
Just know it holds a midnight power.
For in its shade, the legends play,
And all that's silly comes out to stay.

Secrets Beneath the Blossom

In fields of purple, secrets lie,
A squirrel dressed up, oh my, oh my!
He steals the flowers just for fun,
And leaves behind a treasure—a bee in a run!

The bees all giggle; they see the trick,
A dash for pollen, then they're quick!
The flowers whisper tales so bright,
Of silly chases in morning light.

A fox, quite dapper, joins the game,
He wears a crown, oh isn't it lame?
The rumors soar upon the breeze,
As each critter hides with giggles and wheezes.

But when the sun starts to set low,
They gather 'round for a managed show.
With pranks exchanged and stories spun,
In fields of laughter, they've just begun!

Echoes of the Lavender Grove

In the grove, echoes play,
A hedgehog sings in a silly way.
He thinks he's a crooner with quite the flair,
While rabbits dance without a care.

The butterflies join in with cheer,
Spreading giggles far and near.
While a tortoise tries to keep the beat,
With wobbly moves that are quite a feat!

A gnome nearby, with a hat so tall,
Counters the rhythm with a roll and a fall.
Every tumble brings laughter and fun,
As the creatures bask in the day's last sun.

So if you wander where this grove lies,
You'll find the joy beyond disguise.
In echoes that dance and never tire,
They'll fill your heart with pure desire!

Stories in a Lavender Breeze

The breeze brings stories, funny and light,
Of a sheep who dreams of taking flight.
With a paper plane and quite the style,
He aims for clouds with a giggly smile.

A chicken watches from her nest,
Thinking, "Gliding's surely a noble quest!"
While a cat makes bets on who will land,
In a contest deemed completely unplanned.

As laughter drifts through the flowers' hue,
The stories twist and turn anew.
A mouse recites his epic fail,
When he mistook a shoe for a ship's sail!

So listen close to the fragrant air,
It carries mirth beyond compare.
With tales spun wild in every breeze,
Fun times awakened in purple trees!

The Moonlit Lavender Path

Upon the path, the moon shines bright,
With shadows dancing in the night.
A raccoon prances, wearing a mask,
His antics silly—a curious task!

He grabs a flower to play dress-up,
And spills the nectar from a cup.
The bunnies giggle as they hop,
A race 'neath stars that never stop!

An owl hoots wisely from above,
"Dare not disturb the night with love!"
But little do they know, they're quite the crew,
Spreading joy like morning dew!

So stroll the path with joy and cheer,
Where laughter bubbles, loud and clear.
In moonlit tales that tease the heart,
In a world where love and jest impart!

The Myth of the Fragrant Sky

Once a flower tried to fly high,
Tied its petals to a kite, oh my!
But the breeze took it for a ride,
And landed it right in a pot of pie!

The bees giggled, 'What a sight!
A bloom in dessert, how delightfully bright!'
Said the chef, 'This is quite new,
A pie flavored like lavender stew!'

Now folks flock to taste its sweet charm,
But the flower just hopes it won't cause any harm.
After all, who wants to turn into a treat,
When you just want to bloom at your own little street?

So if you see a flower with a grin,
Remember its adventure, and perhaps join in.
Just don't let it taste like cake, my friend,
Or you might find its bloom has come to an end!

Petals of Enchantment

In a meadow where giggles grow,
Petals dance in a whimsical show.
A flower claimed to cast a spell,
But tripped on its roots and fell with a yell!

'Look out!' laughed a butterfly bright,
As the flower's charm turned to flight.
It tangled itself in the air like a fool,
Now it's the star in a garden school!

Gardeners came with their watering can,
Hoping to understand this flowery plan.
But the flower just winked, with a wink and a jig,
'The secret's in laughter, just follow the gig!'

So they laughed till the sun sank low,
And danced with petals in a breezy show.
A flower that fluffed up and brightened the day,
Taught all the gardeners to never dismay!

Aroma of the Lost

In a forest, a scent ran amok,
Claimed to lead to treasure—what a shock!
But the scent was just a flower's sneeze,
Sending squirrels and birds all to their knees!

A gopher exclaimed, 'What a bizarre whiff!
I'm chasing a legend, or an olfactory myth?'
But all that was lurking was a neighboring tree,
Saying, 'It's just pollen; it's pleased as can be!'

The searchers divided in rows and in packs,
Forgotting their maps in the laughter attacks.
No gold, just blossoms, giggles galore,
As they realized they'd found joy to adore.

So if you whiff something strange in the wood,
Don't chase it down, unless you're in the mood.
For laughter's the treasure, as silly as that,
And friendship blooms brighter where humor is at!

The Enigmatic Bloom

There once was a flower with a curious pout,
Whispered secrets no one knew about.
It claimed to be wise, like an old sage,
But mostly just rambled—what a funny page!

The insects would chuckle at each silly tale,
'He said he could fly, but he's stuck on a nail!'
While ants took notes in a tiny book,
The flower just frowned, 'You can't judge a crook!'

'But what do you know?' a ladybug tossed.
'You're just a bloom, pretty, but lost!'
With a flourish, it replied, 'I know how to sway,
And make all of you dance every single day!'

So they broke into laughter and spun around free,
The flower just grinned, 'You're all dancing with me!'
And in that bright moment, all hearts did assume,
Perhaps wisdom is found in the strangest bloom!

Fragrant Echoes

In a field of purple dreams, they prance,
Bees in tuxedos join the dance.
With scents so sweet, they giggle loud,
Even the flowers wear a shroud.

Squirrels in shades with glasses so cool,
Playing hopscotch at the old tree's pool.
The breeze tells jokes as it rustles around,
With every chuckle, joy is found.

A lizard dons a tiny hat,
Strutting like a king, oh, imagine that!
Each petal holds a secret grin,
Tickling toes of creatures within.

So come to this land of giggles so bright,
Where perfume and laughter take flight.
Drop all your cares; let fun ignite,
In fragrant echoes of sheer delight!

Beneath the Lavender Sky

Underneath the violet hue,
Cows wear crowns like it's the new.
Bouncing bunnies play tag in glee,
Clucking hens sing songs of tea.

The sun is a jester, full of cheer,
Throwing bright petals, oh so dear!
With winks and nods from flowers, you see,
Even the weeds join in the spree.

A llama in socks, what a sight,
Playing chess with clouds, oh what delight!
With snorts and guffaws, the day unwinds,
In this quirky world, fun never binds.

So let your worries drift away,
Join the laughter in this play.
Underneath a sky of lavender hue,
We'll dance to the merry tunes anew.

The Serene Veil

Behind the veil of purple mist,
A goat struts by, you can't resist.
Dressed in flair, brilliant and bright,
He winks at flowers, what a sight!

The silence giggles, a playful tease,
While butterflies break dance in the breeze.
In every corner, laughter drips,
Even the daisies take funny trips.

A snail in shades, slow but wise,
Tells tales of the moon in disguise.
With jellybeans that fall like rain,
Each sweet moment brings us gain.

In a land where chuckles reign supreme,
Let these funny fables weave the dream.
With a serene veil wrapped about,
Life's strange wonders turn us out!

A Song of Lavender Night

In the embrace of twilight's glow,
Crickets serenade, stealing the show.
Owl with glasses lifts his brow,
Who knew wisdom could look like that now?

The stars join in with a twinkling laugh,
While fireflies dance, doing the math.
Counting giggles under the moon,
In this silly world, we'll be here soon!

A hedgehog juggles tiny stones,
While frogs croak rhymes in playful tones.
Every ripple in the pond sings,
Of funny events that each night brings.

So under this sky of playful sprites,
Let's sing along with the funny sights.
In the whispers of night, we shall delight,
In a warm embrace till mists take flight!

Dreamscapes in Lavender Hues

In fields where giants dance and sway,
A snail on skis shouts, "Hip-hip-hooray!"
The flowers laugh, they wink and tease,
While bees wear crowns and sip on teas.

A ladybug with shades of green,
Tells stories of a map unseen.
With each small giggle, day turns bright,
A purple wonderland in sight!

Dreams drift by like clouds afloat,
As butterflies don a fancy coat.
Each petal holds a tale or two,
Of frolics bold and silly, too!

So come, my friend, let's skip along,
In hues that make us laugh and strong.
For every whimsy, every cheer,
In dreamscapes wild, there's naught to fear!

Ballad of the Scented Breeze

Oh wind, dear friend, why do you play?
With scents that twirl and sway all day?
You tickle noses, spark a grin,
Dancing through flowers, let chaos begin!

A cheeky squirrel plays the flute,
While bunnies tap with tiny boots.
The breeze, it giggles, whirls and spins,
As crickets join in with their violin sins.

The hedgehog juggles dew drop jewels,
While mockingbirds break all the rules.
Laughter echoes through the air,
In this wild haven, without a care!

So raise a toast to scents that tease,
In our sweet realm of scented breeze.
For life's a song, a silly jest,
Where every moment is a quest!

The Keeper of the Purple Grove

In the purple grove where dreams reside,
A funky frog takes joy in pride.
He wears a crown, a cape so grand,
And rules with laughter through the land.

A sleepy caterpillar's on a chair,
With tales of worms and their affair.
The frog just grins, "Let's make it fun!"
As the sunset dances, day is done.

Of mischief and magic, he's the king,
With every ribbit, the flowers sing.
A circus bright with giggles clear,
In this purple palace, full of cheer!

So come and play, don't be shy,
Let's leap and laugh, let worries fly.
For in this grove of silly glee,
The keeper's charm is wild and free!

Fables Collected in the Fields

Once a mouse with a hat so tall,
Whispered secrets to a grasshopper small.
They spun great tales of courage bright,
Of sneaky ways to steal a bite.

A flower fairy stumbles in,
Her wings caught up in a gusty spin.
With laughter ringing like silver chimes,
She joins the dance of silly rhymes.

Together they share fables to tell,
Of garden quests and the humor swell.
As crickets chirp a jovial tune,
Under the watchful, beaming moon.

So gather 'round, let stories unfold,
In fields where laughter never gets old.
For each fable sung brings joy anew,
In this garden of giggles, just for you!

Whispers of the Purple Dawn

In a field where purple blooms,
The bees all dance and shake like loons.
A snail raced past, his shell so grand,
Proclaiming he was the fastest in the land.

A butterfly swirled, in a flurry of flair,
Claiming he could fly without a care.
A rabbit hopped, with a silly grin,
Said he could run, but only on a whim.

A gossiping crow cawed, loud and clear,
With tales of squirrels that cost a mere.
A wise old tortoise joined the scene,
Said 'slow and steady won't make you keen.'

So here in fields of purple delight,
Every day's a tale, a frolicking sight.
As sunflowers blush, the giggles abide,
Nature's comedy, with none to deride.

Secrets in the Scented Breeze

Whispers float on fragrant air,
While bunnies play without a care.
They tell of cookies, nice and sweet,
Yet only find grass beneath their feet.

A squirrel giggles, hiding his stash,
In a world where mischief makes a splash.
He wears a hat, a flower crown,
Declares himself king of the merry town.

The bees are buzzing, with chatter so loud,
Debating which flower makes them proud.
While a ladybug joins with her tiny legs,
Distracting everyone with endless begs.

Amongst the blooms, the laughter grows,
As everyone shares their funny woes.
In a breeze that tickles, and sways with ease,
Life is a joke, beneath the purple trees.

Enchanted Fields of Violet Dreams

In fields where violets sway and sway,
A frog sings loudly, 'Hip Hip Hooray!'
The daisies join in with a hearty cheer,
While ants march on, all full of beer.

A funny gnome rides on a snail,
Declaring to all, 'I'm on the trail!'
He tells tall tales of giants and trolls,
While the sun shines brightly on their roles.

A curious cat, with a wink and grin,
Lurks around looking for chance to win.
With every pounce, she trips over roots,
Creating chaos in her shiny boots.

So in this realm of whimsy and play,
Every critter brings a comical sway.
In dreams of violet, with laughter in tune,
Fun dances gleefully under the moon.

Tales from the Lavender Fields

In fields of purple, a hare spun round,
Telling tall tales without a sound.
A clumsy wallaby joined in too,
Wobbling about like he had the flu.

With sprightly steps, the birds take flight,
Chasing their shadows, oh, what a sight!
A gathering of frogs croaks a song,
About a snail who's always wronged.

The flowers chuckle at the silly fuss,
As each critter's mishap ignites the bus.
With giggles and snorts, they all agree,
Life's too funny to take seriously!

So here in these fields, where laughter reigns,
Every little hiccup spurs joy and gains.
With colorful blooms reminding us clear,
To find the fun, and hold it dear.

The Aroma of Mystical Memories

In gardens where the flowers chat,
A bee wore goggles, imagine that!
He buzzes tales of wacky bees,
And shares his dreams of tasting trees.

A scent so rich, it tickles the nose,
While garden gnomes strike funny poses.
They dance and twirl in their tiny shoes,
As the silly scent begins to ooze.

A purple cloud floats overhead,
And tickles the toes of a sleeping hedgehog's bed.
He wakes to laugh, spins round and round,
With giggles echoing all around.

So next time you stroll through fields so bright,
Remember the fun that blooms in the light!
With scents that tickle and bees that jest,
A garden of laughter is truly the best!

Shadows of the Swaying Stalks

Swaying under a ticklish breeze,
The flowers tease the bumblebees.
"Don't pick my petals!" they all shout,
As the silly insects dance about.

Each shadow winks, a cheeky sprite,
Bringing laughter almost every night.
The crickets croon a funny tune,
While fireflies giggle and swoon.

In the moonlight, the stalks engage,
In a dance-off, full of laughter and gage.
"Bet you can't sway like me!" they boast,
While the wise old owl giggles with pride, engrossed.

At dawn, they rest in a giggly pile,
With dream-filled sighs and memories a mile.
A day of frolic has come to a close,
In fields where the zest of humor grows!

Beneath the Violet Sky

Beneath a sky of violet dreams,
Where nothing's really as it seems,
A dancing star, all dressed in lace,
Decides to join in the flower race!

The petals prance with floppy hats,
Twirling wild like hyper cats.
They laugh and giggle, "Come join us too!"
While butterflies flutter, painting the view!

A frog in shades starts to croak a beat,
As daisies sway on their little feet.
"Can you keep up?" they tease with glee,
While the frog leaps high, "Just watch me!"

So gather 'round this whimsical sight,
Where silliness reigns under starry night.
With flowers and stars all laughing loud,
It's a hoot! Join the jolly crowd!

Echoes of Lavender's Lullaby

In a field where sweet scents collide,
A serenade from petals wide.
The breeze begins to hum along,
As crickets join in with giddy song.

The older shrubs, with tales to share,
Tell of gigs and whispers in the air.
"Watch out for rabbits with shoes too big,
They hop and trip, doing a jig!"

The daisies declare a laugh fest now,
While a snail brings snacks as he takes a bow.
"Who knew slowness could be so grand?"
As everyone munches and takes a stand.

With echoes of laughter from blooms on high,
They sway and sing under the endless sky.
A night of fun, oh what a sight,
As petals sparkle with pure delight!

The Scented Dreamweaver

In a field where flowers giggle,
Bees wear hats and often wiggle.
A ticklish breeze brings cheeky scents,
Dancing petals, oh such events!

Butterflies don their finest attire,
While the sun plays tunes on a lyre.
Bees invited all to the ball,
But forgot where they parked their wall!

A squirrel juggles acorns and dreams,
Whispering secrets in muffled themes.
Together they bloom in the whimsy,
Creating a joy that's quite dizzy!

So catch a whiff of this grand soirée,
Join the revelry, don't be a cliché.
In this playful patch of pure delight,
Every moment's a blooming good night!

Tales from the Violet Glade

In a glade where violets boast,
Gnomes sip tea and chat with toast.
A frog recites a sonnet bold,
To all who gather, young and old.

Squirrels wear glasses, look quite wise,
Plotting mischief right before our eyes.
They steal the nuts from under their hats,
Exchanging them for singing chats.

Ducks wear bowties, do the cha-cha,
As hedgehogs serve snacks—yummy guava!
A raccoon DJ spins some tunes,
While fireflies dance under the moons.

With every step a chuckle grows,
In this glade where humor flows.
So gather 'round, don't be shy,
The violet tales always fly high!

A Bloom of Memory

In a garden so funny, with twists all around,
A hedgehog named Harry searched for his crown.
He followed a scent, and to his surprise,
Found a dandelion sporting pink ties!

Ladybugs giggled, they rolled in the dew,
Saying, "Harry, your crown is with us, who knew?"
They crowned him with petals, with chatter and cheer,
"Now you're the monarch of this fragrant sphere!"

A snail tells stories of past fragrant days,
How flowers would dance in such whimsical ways.
With laughter erupting from every green bough,
A bloom of memory, here and now.

So don't forget the tale of this plume,
Where laughter and scents always bring room.
With Harry the hedgehog, don't miss your chance,
Join in the garden, and let's laugh and dance!

The Amethyst Harvest

In a patch of purple, what a sight to behold,
A harvest of giggles, stories retold.
A rabbit named Rufus puts on a show,
With carrots for props, he steals the whole flow!

The onions are crying, but they're laughing too,
"Join our brigade, we've got jokes for you!"
The potatoes are rolling with mirth on the ground,
As the clever old tortoise takes first place around.

The crows in the tree are the best of the bunch,
Telling tall tales over their lunch.
"A storm's brewing popcorn!" one squawks with glee,
"Let's harvest the laughter as wild as can be!"

So come to the fields, join the amethyst spree,
Where the fruits of good humor grow naturally.
Each chuckle's a treasure, each giggle's a gem,
In this harvest of laughter, let's join in again!

Threads of the Aromatic Tale

In a field where the colors play,
The bees dance around, they shout hooray!
A scent so strong, it tickles the nose,
With each pluck of flowers, a funny tale grows.

A gnome in a hat, quite round, quite wide,
Falls off a chair, his laughter can't hide.
"I swear it's the flowers!" he chuckles with glee,
"They've built a great castle, just for me!"

With petals as pillows, they dream through the night,
Imagining gardens with colors so bright.
Yet tripping on stems, the garden's a jest,
In this aromatic world, we all feel blessed.

So come, dear friends, join the fun you'll find,
In tales of odd critters, all silly and blind.
For in this great field of giggles and grace,
Even the flowers can't hide their bright face!

Enchantment in Bloom

A wizard with socks, both fluffy and blue,
Danced with the blooms, as wizards will do.
"I cast a great spell of smell!" he did cheer,
While bees laughed and buzzed all around his ear.

A frog leapfrogged in with a flip and a flop,
Landing smack dab in a flower shop.
"Do I smell like a mint?" he croaked quite proud,
As customers giggled, their laughter was loud.

The flowers conspired with voices so faint,
To plot a revenge on a cheeky old saint.
They splashed him with dew in a morning surprise,
As he grumbled and grunted, they giggled in disguise.

So if you're feeling blue in the bloom so bright,
Just recall that the whimsy is out of sight.
For every petal holds laughter, it seems,
In this magical garden of silly dreams!

The Legend of the Lavender Moon

Under the moon, so round and full,
A hedgehog named Larry found a flower bowl.
"What's cooking tonight?" he said with a grin,
As the scent took him on a whimsical spin.

With a whispery sigh, the petals did sway,
Telling tales of mischief in a delicate way.
A raccoon in overalls tried to bake bread,
But mistook it for pie, and toasted his head!

The night critters gathered, all eager to hear,
Of baking gone crazy, filled with good cheer.
With chuckles and snorts, they shared their own tales,
Of blunders and giggles on moonlit trails.

So under the moon, where the strange stories bloom,
Each odd little creature finds laughter to zoom.
In twilight's embrace, they'll dance and they'll croon,
Forever enchanted by the lavender moon!

Whispers in the Lavender Mist

In the midst of the fog, strange whispers arise,
A chicken named Clara wears sparkly ties.
She clucks out a tune that tickles the air,
And rabbits reply in a synchrony rare.

A snail with a top hat gives tips on the best,
Nibbles of greenery, he says with zest.
But tripping on dew, Clara falls with a plop,
And laughs with the rabbits, who just can't stop.

The whispers grow louder, the night softly glows,
As squirrels play pranks, and the mishaps just flow.
Mixing soft scents with giggles and fun,
In the garden's great party, there's room for everyone.

So join in the laughter, don't miss out on the jest,
Where the flowers keep secrets, and humor's the quest.
Among whispers and chuckles, we dance with delight,
In this aromatic mist, all worries take flight!

Transcendence in Bloom

In a field where scents collide,
Bees wear hats, they take pride.
Dancing flowers, what a sight,
Tickling noses, pure delight.

Butterflies with socks so bright,
Fluttering in morning light.
They gossip loud about the breeze,
And tease the frogs up in the trees.

Worms all sport their fancy ties,
As they dig and prep for fries.
The ants, they host a tea affair,
With cucumber sandwiches to share.

Oh, the tales the blooms could tell,
Of silly sprigs that know too well.
From roots to petals, joy unfurls,
In this garden of giggling swirls.

Legends of the Garden Spirits

In the garden, sprites do play,
Telling tales at end of day.
With toadstools for their comfy chairs,
They plot their pranks and giggly dares.

One sprout declared, 'I'll dance tonight!'
But tripped on dew, what a sight.
The flowers laughed, held their sides,
While snails quickly changed their rides.

A gnome on duty lost his hat,
To a mischievous, rolly-polly brat.
He grumbled loud in lopsided shoes,
While ladybugs shared the latest news.

Yet every dusk, with moon aglow,
The spirits sway, putting on a show.
With laughter echoing through the glade,
They weave their magic, never to fade.

The Connoisseur of Color

A painter bee, so quite refined,
Checks every petal, never blind.
With brush and nectar, he creates,
Artful blends that fascinate.

His palette spills from pink to blue,
Sipping nectar, through and through.
He trips on hues, what a blunder!
Bumbles up a storm, oh what thunder!

The flowers gasp, "What's his plan?"
"Will he wear a rainbow skirt, or tan?"
They giggle loud, some hide their grins,
As he splashes color, chaos begins.

Yet in this mess, charm does appear,
With colors that make spirits cheer.
So raise a toast to art in bloom,
To laughter that can fill a room.

Mystical Lilac Veils

In shades of purple, giggles sway,
Behind the bushes where fairies play.
They wrap themselves in fragrant folds,
Whispering secrets, legends untold.

One fairy tripped on her own gown,
Tumbled over, almost crowned.
The flowers wobbled, held their breath,
As laughter danced, evading death.

A gentle breeze, oh what a friend,
Blew the veils, the fun won't end.
While crickets played the night's sweet tune,
The fairies twirled, a whimsical moon.

So join the party, laugh and cheer,
As lilac veils bring magic near.
In this garden, joy prevails,
Where every flower shares their tales.

Tales of the Violet Wanderer

In a field where colors blend,
A wanderer trips on a bend.
With a tumble and a swirl,
He laughs at his toppled world.

His hat flies up into the sky,
A purple bird doth flutter by.
He shouts, 'Is that my new friend?'
As mischief seems to never end.

With a wink and a twirl,
He dances on like a squirrel.
'Oh, what a life! Weightless and bold,
Chasing scents as stories unfold.'

His shoes are stained with dirt and dye,
Each step brings a giggle or sigh.
'Never mind,' he boasts with glee,
'These stains are gifts from the lavender sea!'

Position of Purity

A bottle sits upon the sill,
Claimed to grant a sudden thrill.
He spritzed and spun with childlike cheer,
But smelled like grandma's garden gear!

'What position do I hold,' he says,
'In this fragrant, flowery maze?'
There's purity in his goofy grin,
While bees around him start to spin.

He tries to charm a bumble bee,
But stumbles back, oh dearie me!
With puffs of petals flying high,
He wonders if he can make it fly.

'Position matters not, my friend,
If laughter's what you recommend!
So here's to joy stuck in our toes,
And chuckling at what life bestows!'

Aromas of Ancient Lore

In ancient times, a tale was spun,
Of scents so rich, all thought it fun.
But one young lad, with nose so bright,
Got lost in a whiff one starry night.

His friends declared, 'This smells like cheese!'
Of mysteries that brought them to their knees.
With laughter ringing through the air,
They danced around without a care.

'Oh, find the source!' they called with glee,
'We've got a sniffing odyssey!'
They rolled and tumbled in the grass,
While chasing scents that seemed to pass.

Aroma legends large and wide,
Bring friendship, laughter, and joy inside.
So when in doubt, just take a whiff,
And let your worries gently drift!'

The Wandering Violet

A violet strayed from her patchy home,
Decided to wander and freely roam.
With giggles quickened on the breeze,
She danced along, a sight to please.

She met a fox, who winked quite sly,
'What brings a flower to the sky?'
'Why not,' she laughed, 'it's quite a thrill,
To prance and play on this sunny hill!'

They shared the sun and chased the shade,
A pouncing joy that never swayed.
With petals swirling in a line,
Her heart felt light, her spirit fine.

'I'm the queen of all I see,'
Said she with flair and also glee.
And somewhere, with tacos in the mix,
They laughed away the daily tricks!

The Color of Forgotten Stories

In a field where stories dance,
Colors burst at every glance.
Gossipy flowers, laughing loud,
Wear their hues like a proud shroud.

Whispers of bees fill the air,
Doing the waltz without a care.
Each petal holds a tale or two,
About the things that cats can't do.

Butterflies tell jokes in flight,
Chasing shadows until night.
A quilt of colors on the ground,
Silent laughter all around.

So come and take a gander here,
Where stories bloom and fill with cheer.
Forget your blues, let laughter stay,
In the hues of a vibrant display.

Scented Secrets of the Twilight Grove

In the grove at dusk's embrace,
Silly secrets hide in grace.
Each leaf a giggle, soft and low,
Where even shadows dance and flow.

The roses wear their thorns with pride,
As daisies pull their petals wide.
"Guess who saw a snail run past?"
In a game that's bound to last.

As owls hoot out their witty lore,
The moonlight peeks, then begs for more.
Fragrant whispers, sweet and sly,
A burst of humor in the sky.

Scented laughter floats around,
In this place, fun's always found.
Join the bloom, embrace the night,
With secrets wrapped in sheer delight.

Rituals of the Purple Bloom

Ceremony under the drifting sun,
Where every flower has its fun.
Pollen dances like a ball,
And bees join in, enthralled by all.

They wiggle and waddle, oh so grand,
With tiny capes that just can't stand.
Petals twirl with grand finesse,
As they throw a fragrant mess.

The wind provides a comical tease,
Whispering jokes in rustling leaves.
Among the blooms, you'll find a crowd,
In purple gowns, they're laughing loud.

So join the ceremony today,
Where blooms show off in a funny way.
Forget your worries, sway and spin,
In this colorful, joyful din.

The Guardian of the Floral Realm

In the garden, with giggles and sighs,
Stands a guardian, wise and spry.
With flower crowns atop their head,
Where silly adventures string like thread.

They moonwalk past the fragrant vines,
Chasing butterflies in funny lines.
"Why did the rose cross the way?"
To get to the bloom's bouquet buffet!

The guardian's laughter fills the breeze,
As they perform for buzzing bees.
With every turn, they spin and pose,
Dressed in petals, a sight that glows.

So wander in and take a look,
At this magic garden nook.
With giggles shared beneath the sun,
Where floral wonders invite the fun!

The Spirit of Scent

In a field of purple hue,
The bees all dance and sing,
A flower joked it knew too much,
To be just a simple thing.

A snail slipped by, all out of breath,
Claimed he lost his way,
"With such a smell so sweet and bold,
Who needs GPS today?"

A butterfly, with flair and grace,
Wore shades of violet sky,
Said, "Life's a laugh in this fine place,
All scents surely qualify!"

So if you smell a quirky breeze,
Just know it's nature's jest,
The spirit of the floral tease,
Turns sighs into a jest!

The Ethereal Flower

An ethereal bud once claimed a prize,
For tickling noses near and far,
But when the wind blew with surprise,
It sneezed and caught a spar!

The prize was yet a tiny bug,
Who laughed and danced around,
"I'm not the bloom you thought to hug,
But isn't this fun to be found?"

The flower blushed a shade of blue,
As petals twirled and swayed,
For happiness is often true,
When scents and giggles played.

In gardens where the laughter flies,
The humor blooms on high,
With every whiff that starts to rise,
You'll chuckle 'til you cry!

Fables of the Fragrant Breeze

In tales of scents that trick the heart,
There's one that gets a laugh,
A breeze that makes the flowers part,
For kicks and lots of gaffes.

A squirrel ran past with rumors bold,
That flowers could not speak,
But the breeze just guffawed and rolled,
"Tell me, who's the meek?"

Amidst the blooms, a chatty rose
Said jokes were all the rage,
"Let's prank the hedgehog, I suppose,
And laugh upon this stage!"

Soon fables spread with every gust,
A scent of joy, it swayed,
In fragrant laughs, we put our trust,
And let good times parade!

The Indigo Spell

An indigo magic filled the air,
With giggles drifting wide,
A flower in a wizard's chair,
Slung puns to the sides.

"Look out! I'm casting fun today,
In colors bright and bold!
A spell of laughter on display,
Who knew I'd be so gold?"

The bees nodded in accord,
Each buzz a chuckle shared,
With every flower's prank and hoard,
The garden's joy was bared.

In every petal, tales unfold,
Of humor spun in glee,
This indigo spell, a sight to behold,
Brings smiles for you and me!

www.ingramcontent.com/pod-product-compliance
Lightning Source LLC
Chambersburg PA
CBHW071821160426
43209CB00003B/156